THE OFFICIAL ENGLAND RUGBY ANNUAL 2016

Written by Ben Coles
Designed by Bradley Scott-Peterson

A Grange Publication

© 2015. Published by Grange Communications Ltd., Edinburgh, under licence from the Rugby Football Union. The RFU Rose, the words 'England Rugby' and Ruckley name/image are official registered trade marks of the Rugby Football Union. The Gilbert logo and the Oval / Ellipse trim device is a registered trade mark of Gilbert Rugby.

CANTERBURY and CCC are registered trade marks of Canterbury Limited. Printed in the EU.

Photographs © RFU via Getty Images and Action Images.

ISBN 978-1-910199-60-2

CONTENTS:

WELCOME TO THE OFFICIAL ENGLAND RUGBY ANNUAL 2016

IN THIS YEAR'S ANNUAL we look back on another great year for England Rugby, with Rugby World Cup 2015 to come. Packed full of information on your favourite players, along with great photos, we review England's RBS 6 Nations campaign when they came close to lifting the title on a dramatic last day's action.

We will also take an in-depth look at who England will be facing in the Rugby World Cup group stages when the tournament kicks off this September, from Australia to Uruguay.

Also, we take time to celebrate the success of the England Women's side after their historic Rugby World Cup 2014 triumph, a landmark moment for the sport, along with taking a bigger look at the HSBC World Rugby Sevens Series before the sport takes its bow at the 2016 Olympic Games in Rio after England ensured Team GB's qualification.

That's not all though- there are several games for you to test your knowledge and prove you're England's biggest fan, including quizzes and also 'Spot the ball'!

WE HOPE YOU ENJOY THIS YEAR'S ANNUAL!

RUGBY WORLD CUP 2015

THE RUGBY WORLD CUP IS A SPECIAL MOMENT

for every single fan across the globe and especially for England supporters this time round, as the Rugby World Cup 2015 takes place on home soil!

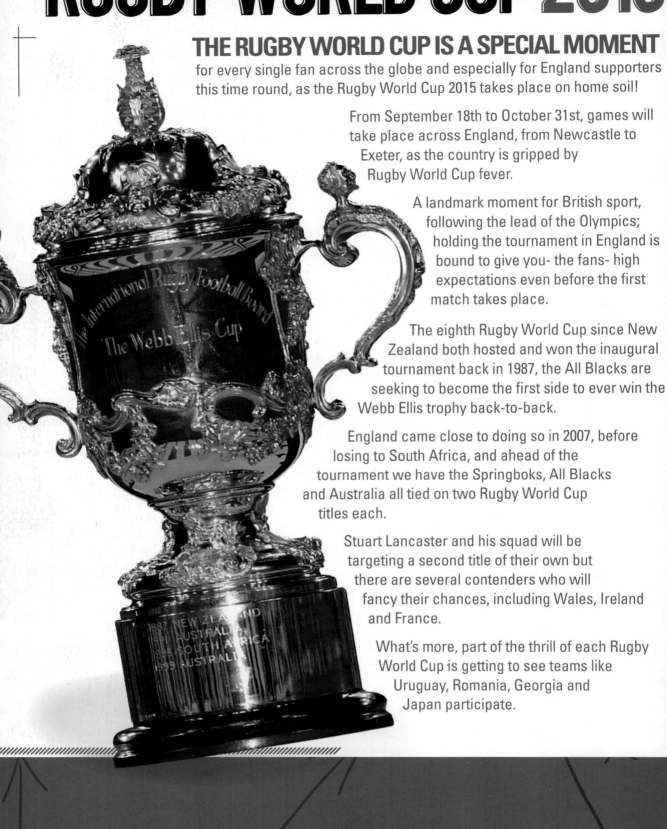

From September 18th to October 31st, games will take place across England, from Newcastle to Exeter, as the country is gripped by Rugby World Cup fever.

A landmark moment for British sport, following the lead of the Olympics; holding the tournament in England is bound to give you- the fans- high expectations even before the first match takes place.

The eighth Rugby World Cup since New Zealand both hosted and won the inaugural tournament back in 1987, the All Blacks are seeking to become the first side to ever win the Webb Ellis trophy back-to-back.

England came close to doing so in 2007, before losing to South Africa, and ahead of the tournament we have the Springboks, All Blacks and Australia all tied on two Rugby World Cup titles each.

Stuart Lancaster and his squad will be targeting a second title of their own but there are several contenders who will fancy their chances, including Wales, Ireland and France.

What's more, part of the thrill of each Rugby World Cup is getting to see teams like Uruguay, Romania, Georgia and Japan participate.

8

RUGBY WORLD CUP WINNERS

1987
(hosted in Australia and New Zealand): New Zealand

1991
(UK, Ireland, and France): Australia

1995
(South Africa): South Africa

1999
(Wales): Australia

2003
(Australia): England

2007
(France): South Africa

2011
(New Zealand): New Zealand

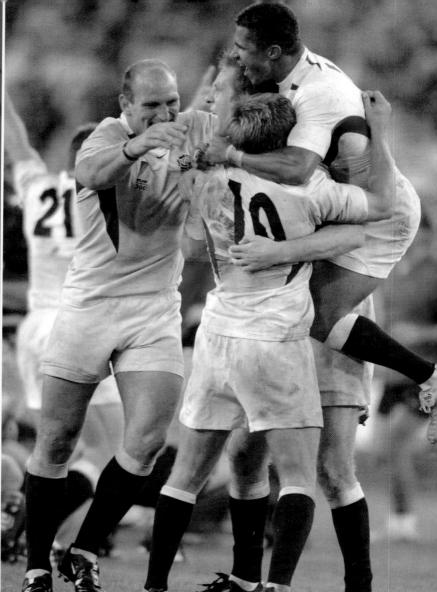

ENGLAND'S POOL OPPONENTS: AUSTRALIA

ONE OF ENGLISH SPORT'S GREATEST RIVALS, Australia, will come up against England in the group stages on the back of winning the Rugby Championship and with plenty of confidence as a result of defeating New Zealand for the first time in four years.

With a squad always packed full of talented players, Australia are always a team to look out for when it comes to international rugby. Having had some ups and downs in the last four years with key figures injured and changes of management, Australia are back on form and playing some great rugby.

Key figures such as David Pocock and Stephen Moore, the team's captain, have suffered with injuries but are now back at the top of their game to the delight of not just Australian supporters, but all rugby fans.

The Wallabies under their third coach in four years, Michael Cheika, are playing their best rugby for some time.

When everyone is fit and firing the Wallabies are a fantastic side to watch and are fully capable of scoring breathtaking tries - helped by the return of overseas-based players Matt Giteau and Drew Mitchell.

Domestic success for the Waratahs, one of the five Australian franchises in Super Rugby, will have also given the national side plenty of confidence with players including Bernard Foley, Michael Hooper and the phenomenal Israel Folau all capable of brilliance.

Arguably one of England's biggest threats in this group, the clash between these two sides is really going to be one to savour.

QUICK FACTS

Nickname: Wallabies
RWC best finish: Winners (1991, 1999)
Captain: TBC
Star Player: Israel Folau
Coach: Michael Cheika

ENGLAND'S POOL OPPONENTS: WALES

FEW GAMES STIR AS MUCH PASSION

in rugby than when England take on Wales with passionate singing and real intensity from both sides which has produced several classic matches throughout history.

Having them paired together in the same Rugby World Cup 2015 pool as Australia means that one of rugby's big sides will not be making it through to the knockout stages - a giant will fall!

Wales will have to face England at Twickenham, having lost their last two matches to England in the RBS 6 Nations home and away, but they have an ace up their sleeve.

No other side has been more successful in the RBS 6 Nations over the last decade than Wales, who have lifted the title four times with three Grand Slams, and we are witnessing a golden generation of Welsh players begin to hit their peak.

Sam Warburton, Leigh Halfpenny, Taulupe Faletau and George North all burst onto the global stage at the 2011 Rugby World Cup 2011 and have gone on to become stars of the sport.

After an agonising semi-final loss in New Zealand four years ago, this might be their time to go the extra mile.

QUICK FACTS

RWC best finish: Third-place (1987)
Captain: Sam Warburton
Star Player: Leigh Halfpenny
Coach: Warren Gatland

KINGS OF SEVENS VERSION OF RUGBY,

Fiji's national side have made real strides in the last few years and will pose a threat at this year's Rugby World Cup 2015, having recently won the Pacific Nations Cup and climbed to 9th in the World Rankings.

For a country with a population of only 950,000 Fijian rugby has given us so many superstars over the years.

Fiji cemented their place in Rugby World Cup history with an amazing win over Wales in the group stages back in France in 2007, knocking the Welsh out of the tournament in the process.

Those heroes from the past like Nicky Little and Sireli Bobo have paved the way for the current squad to shine on the global stage and they have some incredible talents in today's game.

At the top of the pile is Nemani Nadolo. A megastar in Super Rugby for the Crusaders with his tackle-busting runs and impressive pace, Nadolo is also Fiji's goalkicker.

The Islanders will pin their hopes on his fitness and ability to disrupt defences because he has the ability to create something out of nothing.

The general feeling is that Fiji are ready to take on the world under the direction of their new coach John McKee.

When you combine Nadolo with the likes of Niko Matawalu, Asaeli Tikoriotuma, Metuisela Talebula and captain Akapusi Qera, you know that Fiji will be great fun to watch and can cause the likes of England, Australia and Wales real problems.

QUICK FACTS

Nickname: Flying Fijians
RWC best finish: Quarter-final (1987, 1999, 2007)
Captain: Akapusi Qera
Star Player: Nemani Nadolo
Coach: John McKee

ENGLAND'S POOL OPPONENTS: URUGUAY

THE LAST SIDE TO QUALIFY FOR POOL A,
Uruguay are set play in their first Rugby Rugby World Cup in 12 years when they travel to England in September.

Los Teros secured their spot in the tournament after winning a two-legged play-off with Russia to clinch the 20th and final spot in this year's competition.

Winning the second leg 36-27 in front of 14,000 in Montevideo, there were fantastic scenes at the final whistle when Uruguay and their fans knew that the national side would be back at a Rugby World Cup for the first time since 2003.

Ranked 19th in the world, Uruguay will face a tough challenge against England, Australia, Wales and Fiji. Four of their squad play outside of Uruguay and they will unfortunately be without one of their best players for the tournament, the Castres lock Rodrigo Capó Ortega.

However Uruguay will still have some talented players in their side in captain Nicolás Klappenbach and scrum-half Agustín Ormaechea.

Uruguay have won two of their seven Rugby World Cup matches, against Spain in 1999 and Georgia in 2003, and will be hoping to add to that record this September.

QUICK FACTS

Nickname: Los Teros
RWC best finish: Pool stages, 3rd (1999)
Captain: Nicolás Klappenbach
Star Player: Rodrigo Capó Ortega
Coach: Pablo Lemoine

HOST VENUES

Brighton Community Stadium, Brighton
Elland Road, Leeds
Kingsholm, Gloucester
Leicester City Stadium, Leicester
Manchester City Stadium, Manchester
Millennium Stadium, Cardiff
Olympic Stadium, London
Sandy Park, Exeter
St James Park, Newcastle
Stadium MK, Milton Keynes
Twickenham Stadium, London
Villa Park, Birmingham
Wembley Stadium, London

RBS 6 NATIONS REVIEW

IN THE FINAL RBS 6 NATIONS CHAMPIONSHIP BEFORE RUGBY WORLD CUP 2015, Stuart Lancaster gave starts to the exciting young Bath trio George Ford, Jonathan Joseph and Anthony Watson ahead of the first game against Wales, with all three going on to have a major impact on the tournament.

Centred around those three players and thanks to the work of their excellent pack of forwards it was a memorable campaign for England, although they ultimately fell short of lifting the title on points difference.

Ireland's superior total of +63 to England's +57 was the deciding factor as Lancaster's men fell only a converted try short of winning their first title since 2011. So close!

But even though they missed out on the title, they did it in style with a remarkable 55-35 win over France at Twickenham on the final day.

England finished with George Ford as the top points scorer on 75, while Jonathan Joseph was the top try scorer with four, as England won four of their five matches- their only defeat coming away to eventual champions, Ireland, in Dublin.

ROUND ONE - WALES vs ENGLAND

The last time England travelled to Cardiff, in 2013, they were on for a Grand Slam, their first in ten years, but had to defeat Wales in order to make it happen.

So on a Friday night, at the Millennium Stadium in front of a sell-out crowd and in a pulsating atmosphere, England had prepared well to handle the pressure.

After a shaky start when Rhys Webb went over for the hosts, England found their composure and impressed through the dominance of their forward pack, which included a new second row pairing in Dave Attwood and George Kruis.

Anthony Watson scored his first try for England after he won the race to Mike Brown's clever kick through, before Jonathan Joseph danced his way over just after half-time to put England in a position of great control, as Ford sent them into the lead with a penalty.

From there they never looked back, sealing a great 16-21 win.

ROUND TWO - ENGLAND vs ITALY

With morale high, from the win in Cardiff, England returned to Twickenham.

Glimpses of their attacking rugby in Round One had fans excited for more against Italy and the Rose delivered scoring six tries in an impressive 47-17 triumph over the Azzurri.

Jonathan Joseph continued his bright start to the competition with two more tries; the first a brilliant run through the Italian defence as he showed off his pace and footwork, to bring Twickenham to its feet.

It's worth remembering that Italy, in fact, scored first with a try from Sergio Parisse to remind England fans that things wouldn't go all their own way, while there was also major concern for Mike Brown after he went off with a concussion.

England soon found their groove as Billy Vunipola crashed over before Joseph's special try.

A great score for Italy's Luca Morisi kept the contest alive but from there on England were unstoppable, with Ben Youngs, Joseph (again), Danny Cipriani and Nick Easter all going over.

Easter's try was particularly noteworthy, as he became the oldest England player to score in a Test match at 36.

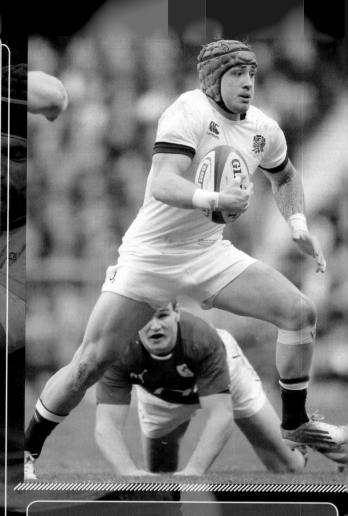

ROUND THREE - IRELAND vs ENGLAND

A big test for England's RBS 6 Nations ambitions was always going to come in Dublin against last year's champions, who have been a rising force in world rugby since the appointment of Joe Schmidt as head coach in 2013.

A tense affair following England's free-flowing display against Italy, the visitors went behind early on after Jonathan Sexton struck two penalties inside the opening ten minutes.

George Ford replied with a drop goal but Ireland proved smarter and more clinical, punishing England for their mistakes, just before half time Anthony Watson was penalised for picking up a loose ball whilst offside. Sexton, the British and Irish Lions number ten, made it 12-3 at half-time.

Ireland more or less confirmed the result not long after the interval with a well-worked try, when Conor Murray chipped over the England defence, down the touchline and Robbie Henshaw won the race to the ball ahead of a back-pedalling Alex Goode.

England fought back with two penalties from Ford, before Jack Nowell was denied a try at the death because of a forward pass. Ireland won 21-9.

ROUND FOUR - ENGLAND vs SCOTLAND

Eager to rebound after their loss in Dublin, there was a swift return for England to Twickenham to face old Calcutta Cup rivals Scotland.

England started with a bang, as Jonathan Joseph scored his fourth try of the campaign with another burst of pace through the Scottish defence.

England created plenty of chances with Mike Brown and Jack Nowell going close but they couldn't cross the line as Scotland's defence held, with the visitors countering with a try from Mark Bennett.

Two penalties from Greig Laidlaw had Scotland ahead at half-time before George Ford coasted through, under the posts, to restore the lead.

A further three points off the tee from Ford put England in control before Mike Brown had a try ruled out for a forward pass by James Haskell. Nowell eventually finished in the corner to round things off but England could have scored more tries, something they would pay for by the end of the tournament, despite winning 25-13.

Lancaster said afterwards: "We scored six tries against Italy and scored three tries today - we should have scored six in this game. It is about composure, execution and patience. The players know that."

ROUND FIVE - ENGLAND vs FRANCE

All eyes were on Twickenham after two extraordinary games in Rome and Edinburgh earlier in the day, as 'Super Saturday' gripped those watching on television and in the stands.

Wales had moved into the top spot after beating Italy, before Ireland did their part by winning with enough points against Scotland to gain the top spot. Which meant it was England's turn, aiming to surpass a target of 26 points to take the title.

In one of the craziest games the RBS 6 Nations has ever seen; there were 12 tries in total from both sides, including seven for England!

They started in a flash with Jonathan Joseph, Mike Brown and George Ford combining to set up Ben Youngs for a try after only 90 seconds; to the roar of the Twickenham crowd.

France however came to play, taking the lead thanks to tries from Sébastian Tillous-Borde and Noa Nakaitaci. They might have been ahead by more had Jules Plisson not been hit and miss off the tee but thanks to penalties from Ford and tries by Anthony Watson and Joseph, England had a 27-15 advantage at the break.

A breathtaking second half then produced 48 points, with each side trading tries as England momentarily held the necessary amount of points before France fought back.

Pushing for the title-winning try in the dying stages, England's rolling maul thundered towards the try line only to be penalised by referee Nigel Owens, crushing their championship hopes. But what a way to fail! It was one of the great games, as England triumphed 55-35.

IN THE SPOTLIGHT

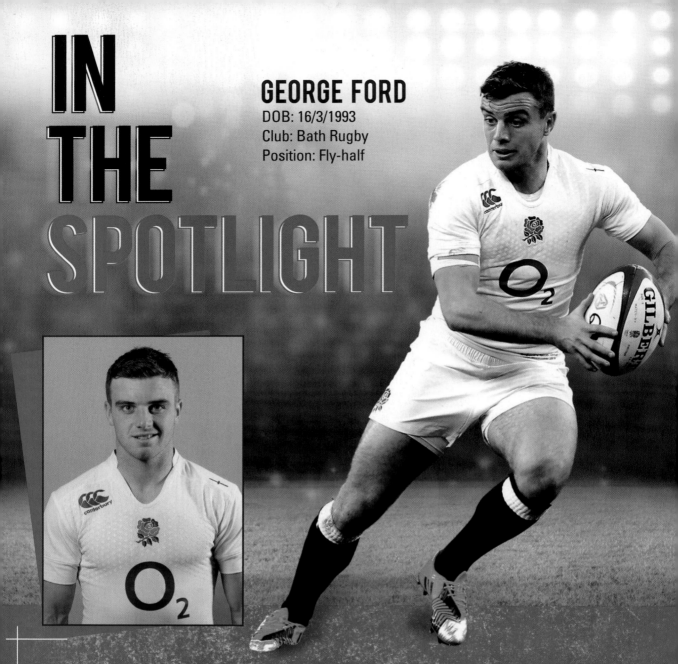

GEORGE FORD
DOB: 16/3/1993
Club: Bath Rugby
Position: Fly-half

ENGLAND'S FLY HALF has enjoyed a fantastic season with his Premiership club Bath Rugby and for his country, ending with him being named as the Aviva Premiership Rugby Player of the Year at the age of 22.

Ford is no stranger to honours having been the first English man to win the IRB Junior Player of the Year award in 2011 and the LV= Young Player of the Year in 2014. On the field he got a runners up medal in the IRB U20 Junior Rugby World Cup 2011 and was English Premiership Champion with Leicester Tigers in 2012/13 season.

On 8 November 2009 he became the youngest Rugby Union player to make his professional debut in England at just 16 years and 237 days old when Leicester Tigers played Leeds Carnegie in the LV=Cup. His debut was doubly notable as his brother Joe was also starting at fly-half for Leeds Carnegie that day.

At the end of the 2012/13 season Ford moved from Leicester Tigers to Bath Rugby where his father, Mike is head coach.

Making his England U18 debut at the age of 15 as fly half in the U20 Six Nations 2011, Ford was awarded man of the match in victories over France, Scotland and Ireland as England won the Grand Slam. Later that year he became the youngest player competing in the U20 Junior Rugby World Cup.

Ford made his senior England debut as a replacement against Wales in the 2014 RBS 6 Nations Championship and his first international

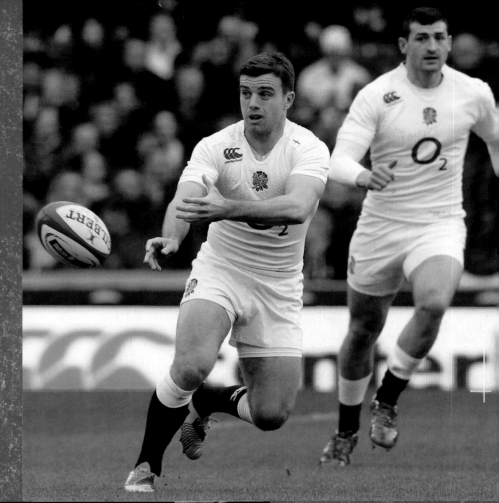

start later the same year against Samoa in the QBE Internationals.

Ford's outstanding club form meant that he retained the England Number 10 shirt for the start of the 2015 RBS 6 Nations finishing as the tournament's top points scorer with 75, which included tries against both Scotland and France.

STUART LANCASTER

COACH PROFILE

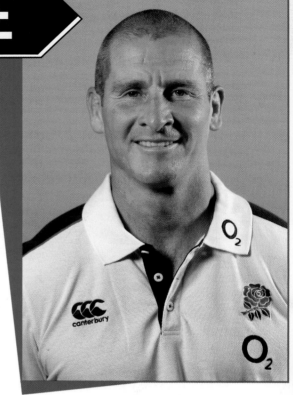

A NEW GENERATION. Stuart Lancaster has built a legacy. The England Head Coach has rebuilt England's image on and off the field. Taking over after a disappointing Rugby World Cup 2011 campaign, the Cumbrian and former school teacher came to the helm as interim head coach before the start of the 2012 RBS 6 Nations Championship.

Lancaster's coaching career began in 2001 as Leeds Carnegie, Academy Manager and later became Director of Rugby at the club in 2006. He joined the RFU as Head of Elite Player Development in 2008, also taking charge of coaching the England Saxons.

In March 2012 following a successful RBS 6 Nations campaign Lancaster was appointed England Rugby Head Coach. Since then England have won 24 of their 39 matches, come second in the RBS 6 Nations on four occasions and defeated New Zealand and Australia. He has turned England into a real contender for Rugby World Cup 2015, whilst bringing through an exciting generation of young talent.

Throughout his time in charge Lancaster has set out to ensure his players are humble and hard-working, while spreading the message and image of the national side all over the country.

With his England side constantly improving ahead of the Rugby World Cup, the decision to appoint Lancaster has certainly been the right one.

QUICK FACTS

Date of Birth: 9 October, 1969
Place of Birth: Penrith, Cumbria
Playing Career: Wakefield RFC,
Leeds Carnegie

Coaching Career: Leeds Carnegie,
England Saxons, England
England Record*: P39 W24 D1 L14
RBS 6 Nations Record*: P20 W16 D0 L4

COACHES PROFILE

ANDY FARRELL OBE *Back Coach*

Having built a successful career in Rugby Union as a player and coach, Farrell is also regarded as one of the greatest British Rugby League players of all time. After a glittering career with Wigan Warriors, Farrell joined Saracens in 2005 and was part of the England squad at the Rugby World Cup 2007. Following his retirement Farrell worked his way up the coaching ladder at Saracens before joining Lancaster's coaching team ahead of the 2012 RBS 6 Nations. He is the father of England fly-half Owen Farrell.

GRAHAM ROWNTREE - *Forwards Coach*

Rowntree is highly regarded across the globe for his expertise at the scrum and after hanging up his boots Rowntree took up a position first with Leicester Tigers then with RFU as National Academy and England Specialist Coach. He became the England Forwards Coach in 2008 and was also the forwards coach for the British and Irish Lions in 2013. He is highly regarded across the globe for his expertise at the scrum.

MIKE CATT - *Attacking Skills Coach*

One of England's most versatile backs and part of the Rugby World Cup 2003-winning squad, Catt spent 12 years at Bath Rugby, racking up 200 appearances and 64 tries. Internationally he won 75 caps for England and toured with the British and Irish Lions in 1997 and 2001. After retiring at the age of 37, following a swansong at London Irish, he became the club's attack coach until 2012 when he moved to join the England set-up under Stuart Lancaster as England's Attacking Skills Coach.

SURPRISING STATS

MOST CAPPED PLAYER

JASON LEONARD OBE - The great England prop forward is still England's most capped player, having played for his country over a 13 year period- from 1991 to 2004. Leonard holds 104 caps during which he only ever scored one try, against Argentina at Twickenham, in 1996.

COMMON FOE

England have faced Scotland more than any other side going all the way back to their first international match in 1871. England's best win during that time came in 2001, when they defeated Scotland 43-3 at Twickenham.

YOUNGEST PLAYER

At just 18 years and 134 days, COLLIN LAIRD made his debut for England against Wales in 1927 – a record that still stands nearly 90 years later. Born in 1908, Laird won ten caps for England and scored five tries.

WORLD RUGBY HALL OF FAME

Ten former England players have been inducted into the World Rugby Hall of Fame for their achievements both on and off the field of play including Rugby World Cup 2003 winning captain MARTIN JOHNSON CBE. The other nine are Alan Rotherham, Harry Vassall, John Kendall-Carpenter, Sir Clive Woodward OBE, Alfred St. George Hamersley, Gill Burns, Carol Isherwood, Jason Leonard OBE and Bill Beaumont CBE.

RANKINGS

England were the number one side in the world when the World Rugby Rankings were introduced back in 2003. They kept that position until 2004, before New Zealand took over at the top. The lowest England have ever been ranked is 8th, back in 2009.

MOST POINTS

JOHNNY WILKINSON CBE - England's 2003 Rugby World Cup hero holds the record for the most Test points scored by an England player with 1179. Wilkinson amassed 239 penalties, 162 conversions, 36 drop goals and six tries during his 13-year international career.

FEARED OPPONENT

New Zealand have been England's toughest opponents throughout history, with the All Blacks defeating the Red Rose on 32 occasions out of 40 matches. There has been one draw – 26-26 back in 1997.

MOST TRIES

RORY UNDERWOOD - Underwood's remarkable record of 49 tries in 85 Tests is unlikely to be beaten by an England player for some time, with the next best being 31 from Ben Cohen and Will Greenwood.

IN THE SPOTLIGHT

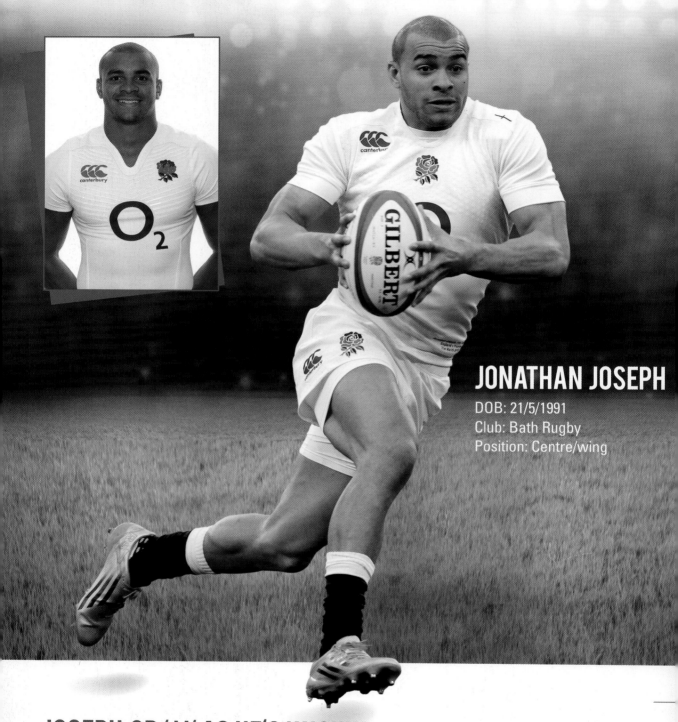

JONATHAN JOSEPH
DOB: 21/5/1991
Club: Bath Rugby
Position: Centre/wing

JOSEPH OR 'JJ' AS HE'S KNOWN, was born in Derby and began playing rugby at the age of 10 for Derby RFC, he was educated at Park House near Newbery - the same schools as Leicester Tigers, England and Lions Flanker Tom Croft, JJ then went onto Millfield in Somerset with England captain Chris Robshaw and loosehead Mako Vunipola, both among his contemporaries.

Joseph, now 24, progressed steadily through the ranks at his first club, London Irish. Coming through the club's academy he made his Premiership debut back in 2009 at the age of 18, before scoring five tries in 13 games the following season. He move to Bath Rugby in season 2013/14 and has not looked back.

For England he played in the age groups progressing from the U18s to U20s. After playing for the Saxons against Scotland A in 2012, he was picked for the senior tour to South Africa that summer. Picking up his first cap off the bench before starting the first two Tests.

Injures set back Josephs international career but after a solid season for Bath Rugby including a sensational try against Toulouse in the European Rugby Champions Cup. Joseph started at 13 for the first game of the 2015 RBS 6 Nations matches against Wales.

Becoming the top try scorer in the RBS 6 Nations 2015 with four, Joseph's memorable season was capped off by being named both the RPA's Player's Player of the Year and England Player of the Year 2015.

GUESS WHO?

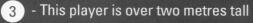

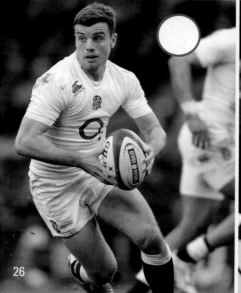

1 - This player was born outside England
- He was born in 1988
- He plays for Northampton Saints

2 - This player kicks at goal
- Is coached by his father at Bath Rugb
- Junior World Player of the Year
  last year

3 - This player is over two metres tall
- Plays for Northampton Saints
- His birthday is in February

4 - This player has a brother who also plays
  prop for England
- He moved from Wasps to Saracens in 2013
- He was born in Brisbane, Australia

5 - This player plays for Leicester Tigers
- He has a brother who plays hooker
- Made his England debut in 2010

(see answers on p.61)

IN THE SPOTLIGHT

WHEN IT COMES TO RUGBY WORLD CUPS,

it's often the kickers who are remembered best.

Joel Stransky, Matt Burke, Jonny Wilkinson, Percy Montgomery and Stephen Donald – each have played a major role in Rugby World Cups over the last 20 years. And now, alongside Wilkinson, England have another hero in Emily Scarratt.

Scarratt was the top points scorer at last year's Women's Rugby World Cup when England put three final heartaches to rest, finishing with 70 points including two tries, one which came in the final.

EMILY SCARRATT

DOB: 08/02/1990
Club: Lichfield
Position: Centre/Fullback

When Scarratt is earning comparisons to Wilkinson and Irish legend Brian O'Driscoll – Scarratt is also an outside centre – you know that she must be a special player.

The 25-year-old from Leicester signed a full-time professional Sevens contract in December 2014 as England's women turn their attention to another big sporting achievement in the 2016 Olympic Games.

Scarratt's natural athleticism has made her stand out not just as a player, but as a role model for any girls who would love to take up the sport.

Turning professional after the Rugby World Cup success was a big moment for the Women's game as Scarratt acknowledged in an interview with BT Sport.

"We knew that we might (go professional) but before the final we didn't dare believe it. The message is massive. Rugby is saying: 'We're taking this seriously'," she said.

"Winning the Rugby World Cup has probably put ourselves on the best ever foundation that we could possibly have had. Now for girls and women to go and take up rugby, they've seen the world champions do it in their own country, so we hope that that is a huge kind of springboard forward."

In the form of Scarratt they certainly have a role model to follow. She has been phenomenal for England and already has over 50 caps, with many more to come.

ENGLAND WOMEN'S
RUGBY WORLD CUP GLORY

FOUR YEARS IS A LONG TIME
to sit on an agonising defeat. England's Women were outstanding at Rugby World Cup 2010, but on home soil they fell short losing to New Zealand 13-10 in the final. It was the fourth straight title for the Black Ferns, a run stretching back to 1998, as England missed out, for the third consecutive final.

By 2014 England had another chance to secure that elusive trophy and a talented side at their disposal to make it happen. In France on August 17, they were finally world champions again.

In France, on August 17, they were finally world champions again.

England arrived in Marcoussis, where the tournament was held with an experienced and exciting squad, spearheaded by the quartet of Maggie Alphonsi MBE, points machine Emily Scarratt, number eight Sarah Hunter and fly-half and captain Katy Mclean.

Not that the talent stopped there. The likes of Rochelle Clark, Tamara Taylor, Jo Gilchrist, Marlie Packer, Kat Merchant and Danielle Waterman were all involved, giving England fantastic depth.

Grouped in Pool A with Canada, Spain and Samoa, England finished the pool stages unbeaten, drawing 13-13 with the Canadians in the final group game.

Defending champions New Zealand hadn't made it out of the pool stages after their shock loss to Ireland, who became England's semi-final opponents in the process.

Up against an Irish side with three wins from three games and their excellent full-back Niamh Brigg, England went behind 7-0 but then scored 40 unanswered points, with five tries, to march into the last four.

Victory meant England took on Canada in the final, their pool opponents who had knocked out hosts France thanks to a magical solo try from winger Magali Harvey.

England were determined to go one step further than 4 years ago and lift the trophy.

Two penalties from Scarratt and a try from Waterman put them in control at half-time leading 11-3, but two penalties from Harvey closed the gap to just two points as England's composure was tested.

They pulled through – Scarratt adding a third penalty and then sealing an emotional win for the players and their coach Gary Street, as England triumphed 21-9.

Champions once again for the first time since 1994, Katy Mclean stepped forward to take the trophy from World Rugby chairman Bernard Lapasset sparking wild celebrations both in Paris and back home.

Not forgetting the pain of the previous finals, Mclean was quick to mention those players who had fallen at the final hurdle before.

"We've worked so hard for this, and there are so many great legends that have gone before us that haven't won this in an England shirt, and that's for all of them who are here today."

MISSION ACCOMPLISHED!

SPOT THE BALL

Can you work out which is the real ball in the picture below?

(answer on p.61)

1

2

3

4

5

6

STARS OF THE FUTURE

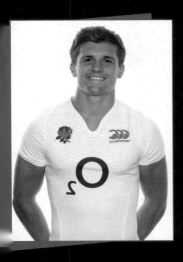

HENRY SLADE

One of the promising group of young players hailing from Exeter Chiefs, Slade's versatility on the back of a strong season may just push him into contention for a spot in England's final Rugby World Cup 2015 squad.

What has made the 22-year-old really stand out over the last year or two has been his composure. Little flusters Slade and as a result the teams around him – be it Exeter or the England U20s.

Born in Plymouth, Slade spent valuable time on-loan at his hometown club, Plymouth Albion, during the 2011/2012 season while making his way through the ranks with the England U18 and U20 sides.

Slade drew comparisons with England number ten Toby Flood and since his Premiership debut against London Irish in April 2013 he has been a vital player for the Chiefs.

His first senior appearance for England came in a 2014 match against the Barbarians at Twickenham when Slade shone with the boot and the ball in hand.

Slade's consistent 2014/2015 season resulted in him being involved in England's 50-man preliminary Rugby World Cup training squad. In August 2015, in the QBE International against France, he won his first Test cap.

Sir Ian McGeechan, the British and Irish Lions legendary player and coach, said this about Slade in a column for the Telegraph: "I like him as a player because he seems to score points at key times. I have seen him score vital points when the game is in the balance. It is something that is easily overlooked.

"Slade appears to have so much more time on the ball, never being rushed, a sure sign of a quality player in any sport. He makes good decisions."

High praise indeed.

IN THE SPOTLIGHT

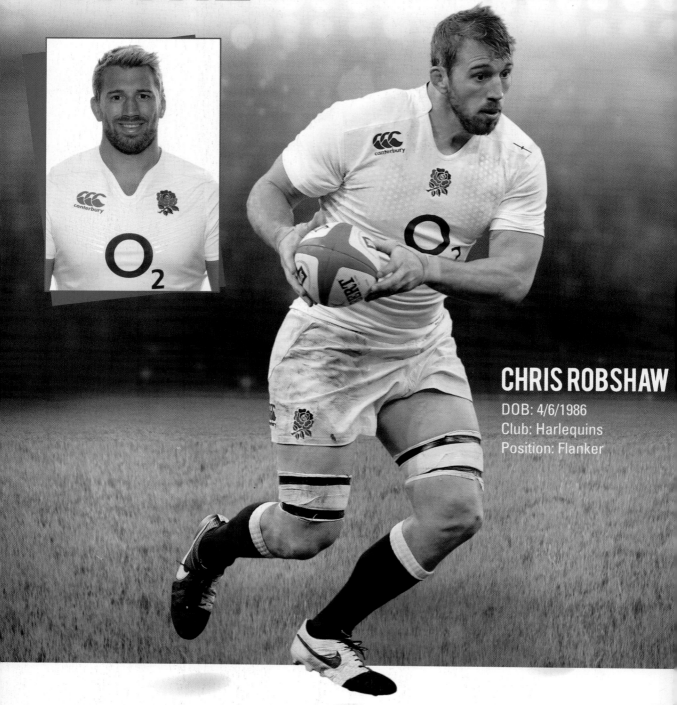

CHRIS ROBSHAW

DOB: 4/6/1986
Club: Harlequins
Position: Flanker

HARLEQUINS FLANKER CHRIS ROBSHAW has gone from narrowly missing out on the Rugby World Cup 2011 squad to being England's outstanding captain, since Stuart Lancaster took over in 2012.

Robshaw, who captained the first XV while at school, went on to make his Harlequins debut in 2007 at the season-opening Double Header and has since gone on to make over 200 appearances for the London club.

The highlight of Robshaw's club career has, undoubtedly, been leading Harlequins to the Aviva Premiership title in 2012.

Robshaw had only won a single cap for England, in 2009 against Argentina, before his first Test as captain against Scotland at the start of the 2012 RBS 6 Nations.

England have gone on to win 21 of their 36 Test matches with Robshaw at the helm. He has also scored two tries for his country – against Australia in 2013 and Italy in 2014.

Now he faces his biggest challenge yet in guiding England to Rugby World Cup 2015 glory on home soil.

Robshaw is set to overtake the great Martin Johnson on the all-time list for the number of games leading England as captain, putting him only behind Will Carling.

With his authoritative leadership and huge tackling figures, including 26 in one game against Wales, Robshaw is playing some of his best rugby. You sense, however, there is more to come.

ENGLAND QUIZ

KNOW YOUR RUGBY HISTORY OR THE SIZE OF TWICKENHAM STADIUM?

Here are 15 questions for you to work your brains around *(hint: all the answers are in the annual!)*

1. HOW MANY PLAYERS are on each rugby team including replacements?

2. IN WHICH YEAR did New Zealand host and win the first ever Rugby World Cup?

3. WHAT IS THE MAXIMUM CAPACITY of Twickenham stadium?

4. WHO CAPTAINED the England Womens side to Rugby World Cup glory in 2014?

5. WHAT IS the Australia rugby team's nickname?

6. WHICH CLUB does England star Jack Nowell play for?

7. WHO IS the men's England Sevens head coach?

8. ENGLAND FIRST PLAYED Scotland in which year?

9. IN WHICH COUNTRY was England winger Marland Yarde born?

10. WHICH STADIUM will be used to host Rugby World Cup matches in Newcastle?

12. ENGLAND CAPTAIN Chris Robshaw was born in which year?

13. WHICH PLAYER has scored the most ever international tries for England?

14. WHICH COUNTRY has won the most Rugby World Cups?

15. WHICH SIDE knocked England out of the 1999 Rugby World Cup?

16. WHICH TWO PLAYERS scored two tries each when England defeated France 55-35 in the Six Nations?

(Answers on p.61)

IN THE SPOTLIGHT

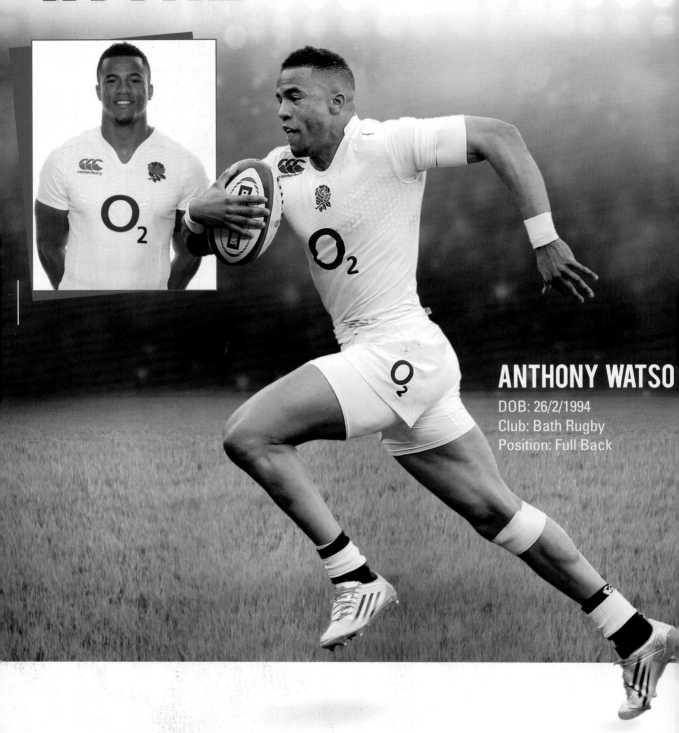

ANTHONY WATSO

DOB: 26/2/1994
Club: Bath Rugby
Position: Full Back

ANTHONY WATSON'S RUNNING WITH THE BALL in hand, and all-round composure for someone so young makes him an exciting prospect.

Anthony, 21, was born in Ashford, Middlesex, and was an early starter in the game at Effingham & Leatherhead RFC at five. From there he advanced into the England U16 and U18 sides as well as becoming vice-captain at his school, St George's College in Weybridge, where he studied chemistry, economics and PE. Anthony was also in St George's Junior School U8 team that won the national title.

He made his A League debut for London Irish against Bath in October 2010 becoming their youngest player to appear for the first team. Watson had also been a member of Wimbledon Football Academy and had trials for Chelsea.

With a Junior U20 World Championship and U20 Six Nations Championship to his name Watson joined Bath Rugby in 2013.

A newcomer to England's squad for the 2014 RBS 6 Nations Championship. His debut was off the bench against New Zealand at Twickenham last November. He also started on the right wing against South Africa, Samoa and Australia that month. Anthony's maiden try against Wales at the Millennium Stadium in February this year rewarded his quick thinking and precision when he pounced on a Mike Brown grubber kick over the line.

He started all five RBS 6 Nations matches in 2015 and scored a second try in the 55-35 win over France at Twickenham in the final game. Two tries in the first 17 minutes in the QBE International against France at Twickenham in August thrilled the crowd and gained him QBE Man of the Match.

Athleticism and pace are the shining assets and with so much potential, it will be fascinating to see what Watson can achieve.

STARS OF THE FUTURE

JAMIE GEORGE

poached three tries in four games for England U18, went on to appear 20 times for the U20 side and played in the Junior World Championship in 2009 and 2010. He captained London & South-East U16 and the Saracens A team, the Storm.

Richard Hill, the former England back row, and Mike Hynard have mentored him at Saracens, where he respects South African hooker Schalk Brits. Jamie says: "He is a fantastic role model. I admire his approach to life and rugby and I have so much to learn from him. "

George is one of the three hookers named in the final squad of 31 ahead of the Rugby World Cup 2015.

Making the final England group of 31 wasn't easy, but George has finished the season at a canter and got his England debut off the bench in Paris in August in England's loss to France.

They say that when it comes to winning selection for internationals, it's all about timing. If that's true, then people should be asking Jamie George for advice.

George has been a mainstay in the Saracens team this season, a young gun in a pack which looks increasingly youthful with Mako and Billy Vunipola, George Kruis, Jackson Wray, Will Fraser and Maro Itoje all involved.

Born in Welwyn Garden City, Jamie first laced up his boots when five at Hertford RFC,

ENGLAND WERE GOING FOR A HAT-TRICK of U20 level successes when they travelled to Italy to compete in the 2015 U20 World Championship.

A number of players from the last two Championships have gone on to excel in the senior game whether for club or country, including Jack Nowell, Henry Slade and last year's captain Maro Itoje.

The bar had therefore been set for the 2015 squad which itself included a number of quality prospects, from captain Charlie Ewels to flanker Lewis Ludlam and exciting backs Rory Jennings and Aaron Morris.

England were pooled with France, Wales and Japan in Pool A and got off to a bright start in their opening game, picking up a 59-7 victory over Japan with two players, Morris and scrum-half Stuart Townsend, scoring twice as England finished with nine tries to their name.

Four days later and at the same venue in Calvisano, England were back in action against Wales. England started well with 3 tries in the first half hour which gave Wales too much to do.

Four tries from England meant they secured a 30-16 bonus point win to sit on a maximum ten points from their first two matches, putting them level with France.

The winner of the Anglo-French clash would top Pool A and potentially secure a stronger draw in the semi-finals, but England started slowly. Two tries from Damien Penaud left them chasing the scoreboard and they couldn't recover in time, going down 18-30 to leave

Jon Callard's side with a nervous wait to see if they would qualify as the fourth seed for the semi-finals.

Neither Australia nor Ireland were able to secure the necessary bonus point to knock England out of the fourth seed slot, meaning England advanced to the semi-finals to face the side they defeated in the 2014 final, South Africa.

The Junior Boks came into the knockout stages with an undefeated record but England showed great maturity and composure as they ground out a 28-20 victory to go through to the final. Two late tries from South Africa added some respectability to the scoreboard, but England were comfortable winners.

The dream of winning three straight titles remained alive for England but they faced New Zealand in the final, who were going for their first title since 2011.

Despite scoring the first try through Max Clark, New Zealand's power told, and through their outstanding number eight Akira Ioane they triumphed 21-16.

England lost the match, but their players did their country proud and look set to be stars of the future after another strong World Rugby U20 Championship.

CONSIDER YOURSELF AN EXPERT ON RUGBY'S RICH HISTORY?

Here are some landmark moments and facts from the sport we love that you may not be aware of.

DID YOU KNOW?

FAMOUS RUGBY PLAYERS

You might be surprised, but over time rugby has been played by Presidents of the United States and Hollywood actors to name a few celebrities. George W. Bush was a full-back at Yale University, while George Clinton was a prop at Oxford! Then there's Daniel Craig (currently James Bond) and Javier Bardem, who was good enough as a flanker to play for Spain U21s.

THE GLOBAL GAME

As of 2015, there have been 25 sides that have participated in the Rugby World Cup since the first tournament took place in 1987. Four of those teams have appeared only once - Portugal (2007), Russia (2011), Spain (1999) and Ivory Coast (1995).

GUY THE GREAT

The world's oldest rugby club was started right here in England. Guy's Hospital RFC was created in 1843 but a merger of hospitals with nearby St Thomas's Hospital in the 1980s also merged the two clubs.

LOWLY TRIES

Scoring tries might now be the best way of gathering points – five to be exact, seven with a conversion – but before the 1890s a try was only worth a single point, changing to two points in 1891 and three points in 1893.

EARLY CROWD

Back in 1910, 18,000 fans packed into Twickenham to watch England face Wales in the stadium's first ever international match. Today, Twickenham holds a capacity of 82,000!

THE PRICE IS RIGHT

Of course prior to their first Test match, the RFU had to buy the land. Just over £5,500 was paid back in 1907 to purchase the farmland where Twickenham now proudly stands.

IN THE SPOTLIGHT

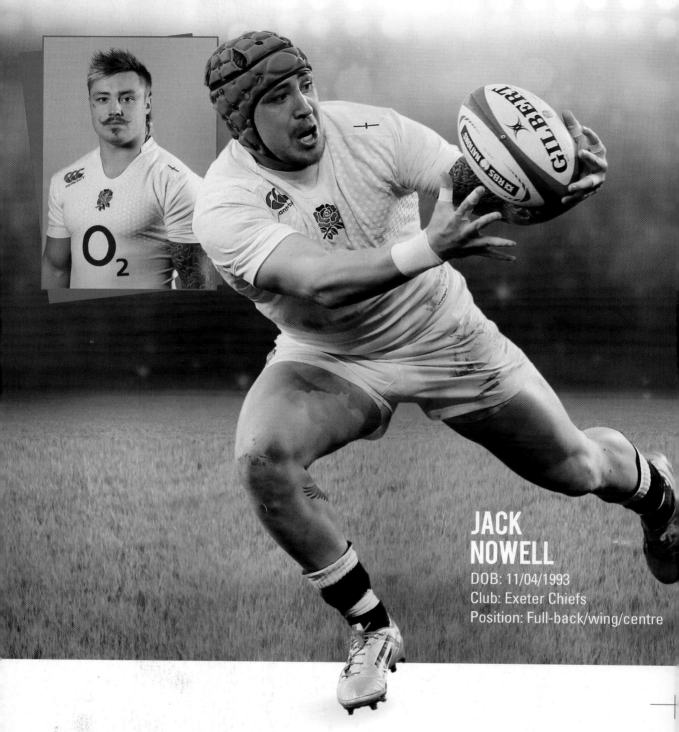

JACK NOWELL
DOB: 11/04/1993
Club: Exeter Chiefs
Position: Full-back/wing/centre

WHEN BROWSING THROUGH AN ENGLAND
squad photo, Jack Nowell is hard to miss with his individual style.

Though, as anyone who has watched Nowell plays knows, there are a lot of things that make this particular England player unique.

Nowell was born and raised in Cornwall, learning his trade in at Cornish Pirates before making a huge impression with the England U20 side.

He was a try scorer in the 2013 Junior World Championship Final when England defeated Wales. Such was the impression he made during the tournament that in August, that same year, he was promoted to the England Saxons.

A string of exciting performances for Exeter culminated in him starting on the wing for England in the first match of the 2014 RBS 6 Nations, going on to play in all five games and scoring his first Test try against Italy.

Injuries denied him a chance to play in that year's November Tests but he returned half-way through the 2015 RBS 6 Nations to score three tries in two games against, Scotland and France.

Nowell's versatility makes him a huge asset to England, with the 22-year-old able to line up a full-back, wing or outside centre.

He has been praised in the past for his toughness despite only being 5ft 10, but Nowell's bravery can't be questioned.

HSBC WORLD SEVENS SERIES REVIEW

THIS YEAR'S HSBC WORLD SEVENS SERIES

held extra importance for all those involved with the prospect of automatically qualifying for the 2016 Olympic Games up for grabs as well as the title.

Only the top four would secure their spot in Rio, with the battle for those places going right down to the final rounds.

The England men's side was selected to represent Great Britain in this year's HSBC World Sevens Series, meaning that if they finished in the top four then Team GB would qualify.

The make-up of the squad for Rio, which will consist of players from England, Scotland and Wales, will now be decided, along with a coach and captain.

The series this year took place in Australia, the UAE, South Africa, New Zealand, USA, Hong Kong, Japan, Scotland and England, finishing up at Twickenham on a packed weekend full of space-themed fancy dress!

England started the season brightly, finishing third at the Gold Coast Sevens, before they struggled in Dubai and Port Elizabeth.

England then came so close to success next time out in Wellington, where they narrowly lost in the final to New Zealand but picked up valuable points.

Unfortunately, there was more disappointment to follow in Las Vegas and Hong Kong, before England were brilliant in Japan, defeating South Africa 21-14 in the final for their first title of the season.

That success in Tokyo provided England with both required points and also a shot of confidence, on which to finish the campaign.

They performed strongly in Glasgow and Twickenham, finishing third and fourth respectively, to secure that fourth place in the table, 12 points ahead of their nearest rivals Australia.

Throughout the season, captain Tom Mitchell was outstanding. He finished with 216 points and was at the heart of their attacks throughout. He was also the only England player to be named in the official season's Dream Team.

England coach, Simon Amor spoke with immense pride following the side's qualification for Rio, while also looking ahead to the future.

"I am so proud of the boys. They have worked so hard this year and there have been some real challenges, but they have kept their mental focus and managed all the expectations.

"We have had a few rocky bumps along the way, but the work ethic from the team and leadership from Tom Mitchell has been great. I am so proud of them.

"This is a very special and exciting group. I am excited about what this group can do in the future."

Meanwhile, there was also success for the England women's side, who made sure of their qualification at the Amsterdam Sevens tournament in May.

A crucial third-place playoff win over the United States in the final tournament saw them edge out the Americans to the fourth automatic qualification spot.

The 15-14 win for England left both sides tied on 76 league points, with England's points difference counting in their favour. Just like the Men's side, by finishing fourth England's Women booked Team GB's spot in the Olympics.

A HUGE WELL DONE TO BOTH TEAMS!

FLASHBACK: 1999 RWC

IT'S BEEN 16 YEARS since a Rugby World Cup match was played in England, making this year's tournament all the more exciting for a new generation of fans who were too young or not yet born, the last time we saw teams contesting for the Webb Ellis trophy on English soil.

Just as there will be in September, 20 teams took part in games across the UK, Ireland and France to win only the fourth ever Rugby World Cup tournament, with South Africa coming to Europe as the holders.

England faced a tough group stage being paired with New Zealand, Italy and Tonga but all of their pool matches were played in England. With one of England, Scotland, Wales, Ireland and France in each of the pools, the matches were then played in the respective countries.

The All Blacks and England had no problems against Italy or Tonga, but it was New Zealand who triumphed 30-16 when the two teams played in front of 72,000 at Twickenham, with Jonah Lomu

among the Kiwi try scorers.

As a result, England finished the group stages as runners-up, putting them into a quarter-final play-off against Fiji which they won 45-24.

New Zealand, South Africa, France, Wales and Australia all qualified for the quarter-finals outright; with England, Scotland and Argentina joining them after winning their play-off matches with Fiji, Samoa and Ireland.

England travelled to Paris to face South Africa in the quarter-final but they were well beaten by South Africa- 44-21, with the Springboks fly-half Jannie du Beer landing a record five drop goals in a single game to go with five penalties and two conversions.

Australia, New Zealand and France also advanced to the last four, meaning that les Bleus were the only northern hemisphere side left in the competition.

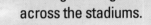

Two epic semi-finals followed. The first saw Australia defeat South Africa in extra-time, after a tryless encounter was won by Matt Burke kicking eight penalties, plus a Stephen Larkham drop goal against six penalties plus a drop goal from De Beer, meaning the Wallabies won 27-21.

The other semi-final at Twickenham is regarded as one of the greatest World Cup games of all time, with France defeating the All Blacks 43-31, to meet Australia in the final.

A one-sided affair in Wales, Burke's boot was the key again as the full-back kicked seven penalties to go with two tries from Ben Tune and Owen Finegan for the Wallabies, to win their second World Cup trophy, after first triumphing in 1991.

Lomu, who was brilliant in the quarter-final and semi-final, finished as the top try scorer with eight, while Argentina's Gonzalo Quesada was the tournament's overall top points scorer with 102.

With Australia the winners and France the runners-up, South Africa took third place after defeating New Zealand 22-18, with a combined 1.75 million people watching all the games across the stadiums.

MARTIN JOHNSON

"MENTAL PREPARATION IS CRUCIAL FOR SUCCESS"

He is one of the greatest second rows to have ever played the game, and also one of its most respected captains. Whether with Leicester, England or the British and Irish Lions, Martin Johnson was an exceptional leader and right at the core of England's Rugby World Cup 2003 success when he lifted the Webb Ellis Cup in Sydney.

Eight years later, Johnson was back in charge of England but this time as a head coach, not as captain, when he took his country to the Rugby World Cup 2011 in New Zealand.

There was to be no repeat of the 2003 success for Johnson but his experience of having been involved in four Rugby World Cups - three times as a player in 1995, 1999 and 2003 - make any words of advice worth their weight in gold.

Johnson, who scored two tries for England in his 84 appearances between 1993-2003, expects that hosting the Rugby World Cup on home soil will provide unique challenges for Stuart Lancaster and his players.

"A home tournament is a double-edged sword in many ways, living with the expectation, the demands, the media and everything else. It sounds obvious, but you just have to remember that it's about playing the game," Johnson said in June when he revealed the ticket designs for this year's Rugby World Cup, which include pictures of him and four other Rugby World Cup winning captains - Francois Pienaar, John Eales and Richie McCaw.

Johnson points out that all of the teams will be up to scratch physically for the tournament, but it will be the mental preparation from each side that could prove to be the big difference between success and failure.

"All the teams at the Rugby World Cup will be physically fit, but it's about being mentally in the right place." Throughout his career Johnson amassed a remarkable collection of winners medals. There were five Premiership titles with Leicester Tigers and two European Cups. Then five RBS 6 Nations titles, including two Grand Slams, the World Cup 2003 triumph and a victorious Lions tour in 1997 against South Africa. Few players can boast that level of success.

There will be a handful of contenders at this year's Rugby World Cup, but only one side can win. In Johnson's mind, with all his experience of success, the side who comes out on top, however many individual talents they have, will be able to come together to drive their way to success as a united force.

"Normally at each World Cup there are four or five teams that can win it. But you need that collective will to go all the way, to handle the pressure and get over the line. That's the key ingredient."

If England can remember that then they might be world champions once again.

ENGLAND 2014-2015 MATCH STATS

ENGLAND 21 - 24 NEW ZEALAND
Twickenham, November 8

England:
Tries: May, Penalty try
Conversions: Ford
Penalties: Farrell 3

New Zealand:
Tries: Cruden, McCaw, Faumuina
Penalties: Cruden 2, Barrett

ENGLAND 28 - 31 SOUTH AFRICA
Twickenham, November 15

England:
Tries: Wilson, Morgan, Barritt
Conversions: Farrell 2
Penalties: Farrell 2, Ford

South Africa:
Tries: Serfontein, Reinach, Burger
Conversions: Lambie 2
Penalties: Lambie 3
Drop Goal: Lambie

ENGLAND 28 - 9 SAMOA
Twickenham, November 22

England:
Tries: May 2, Brown
Conversions: Ford 2
Penalties: Ford 3

Samoa:
Penalties: Pisi 3

WALES 16 - 21 ENGLAND
Millennium Stadium (Cardiff), February 6

Wales:
Tries: Webb
Conversions: Halfpenny
Penalties: Halfpenny 2

England:
Tries: Watson, Joseph
Conversions: Ford
Penalties: Ford 3

ENGLAND 26 – 17 AUSTRALIA

Twickenham, November 29

England:
Tries: Morgan 2
Conversions: Ford 2
Penalties: Ford 4

Australia:
Tries: Foley, Skelton
Conversions: Foley 2
Penalties: Foley

ENGLAND 47 – 17 ITALY

Twickenham, February 14

England:
Tries: B Vunipola
Joseph 2, B Youngs,
Cipriani, Easter
Conversions: Ford 3,
Cipriani
Penalties: Ford 3

Italy:
Tries: Parisse, Morisi 2
Conversion: Allan

IRELAND 19 – 9 ENGLAND

Aviva Stadium (Dublin), March 01

Ireland:
Tries: Henshaw
Conversions: Sexton
Penalties: Sexton 4

England:
Penalties: Ford 2
Drop Goal: Ford

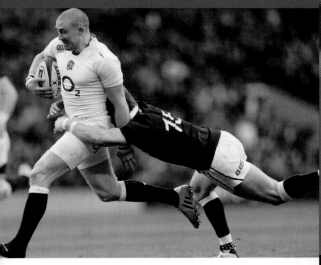

ENGLAND 25 – 13 SCOTLAND

Twickenham, March 14

England:
Tries: Joseph, Ford,
Nowell
Conversions: Ford 2
Penalties: Ford 2

Scotland:
Tries: Bennett
Conversions: Laidlaw
Penalties: Laidlaw 2

ENGLAND 55 – 35 FRANCE

Twickenham, March 21

England:
Tries: B Youngs 2, Watson,
Ford, Nowell 2, B Vunipola
Conversions: Ford 7
Penalties: Ford 2

France:
Tries: Tillous-Borde,
Nakaitaci, Mermoz,
Debaty, Kayser
Conversions: Plisson 2
Penalties: Plisson, Kockott

ENGLAND RUGBY

Player's statistics as of 27/08/2015

CENTRE

PROP

FULL BACK

CENTRE

BRAD BARRITT

Club: Saracens
Height: 1.85m
Debut: v Scotland
Points: 10
Position: Centre
Weight: 96k
Caps: 22

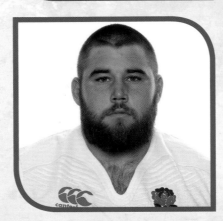

KIERAN BROOKES

Club: Northampton Saints
Height: 1.88m
Debut: v New Zealand
Points: 0
Position: Prop
Weight: 124kg
Caps: 11

MIKE BROWN

Club: Harlequins
Height: 1.83m
Debut: v South Africa
Points: 30
Position: Full Back
Weight: 92kg
Caps: 38

SAM BURGESS

Club: Bath Rugby
Height: 1.93m
Debut: v Fance
Points: 0
Position: Centre
Weight: 116kg
Caps: 1

PLAYER PROFILES

DANNY CARE

Club: Harlequins
Height: 1.77m
Debut: v New Zealand
Points: 44
Position: Scrum Half
Weight: 87kg
Caps: 52

DAN COLE

Club: Leicester Tigers
Height: 1.91m
Debut: v Wales
Points: 5
Position: Prop
Weight: 118kg
Caps: 51

OWEN FARRELL

Club: Saracens
Height: 1.88m
Debut: v Scotland
Points: 294
Position: Fly Half
Weight: 92kg
Caps: 30

GEORGE FORD

Club: Bath Rugby
Height: 1.78m
Debut: v Wales
Points: 119
Position: Fly Half
Weight: 84kg
Caps: 12

SCRUM HALF

PROP

FLY HALF

FLY HALF

ENGLAND RUGBY

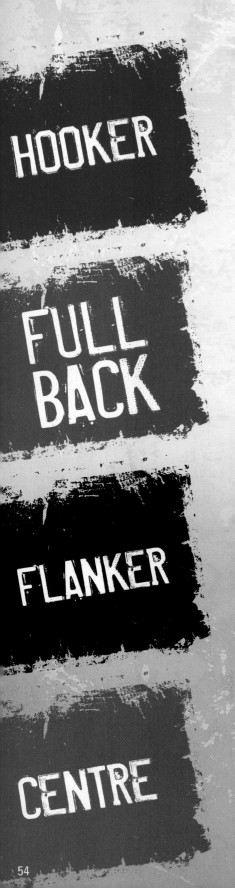

HOOKER

JAMIE GEORGE

Club: Saracens
Height: 1.83m
Debut: v France
Points: 0
Position: Hooker
Weight: 109kg
Caps: 1

FULL BACK

ALEX GOODE

Club: Saracens
Height: 1.80m
Debut: v South Africa
Points: 3
Position: Full Back
Weight: 91kg
Caps: 18

FLANKER

JAMES HASKELL

Club: Wasps
Height: 1.94m
Debut: v Wales
Points: 20
Position: Flanker
Weight: 114kg
Caps: 60

CENTRE

JONATHAN JOSEPH

Club: Bath Rugby
Height: 1.83m
Debut: v South Africa
Points: 25
Position: Centre
Weight: 90kg
Caps: 12

PLAYER PROFILES

GEORGE KRUIS

Club: Saracens
Height: 1.98m
Debut: v New Zealand
Points: 0
Position: Lock
Weight: 113kg
Caps: 8

LOCK

JOE LAUNCHBURY

Club: Wasps
Height: 1.96m
Debut: v Fiji
Points: 10
Position: Lock
Weight: 118kg
Caps: 23

LOCK

COURTNEY LAWES

Club: Northampton Saints
Height: 2.00m
Debut: v Australia
Points: 0
Position: Lock
Weight: 111kg
Caps: 39

LOCK

JOE MARLER

Club: Harlequins
Height: 1.84m
Debut: v South Africa
Points: 0
Position: Prop
Weight: 110kg
Caps: 32

PROP

ENGLAND RUGBY

WINGER

NO.8

WINGER

LOCK

JONNY MAY

Club: Gloucester Rugby
Height: 1.88m
Debut: v Argentina
Points: 20
Position: Winger
Weight: 90kg
Caps: 15

BEN MORGAN

Club: Gloucester Rugby
Height: 1.91m
Debut: v Scotland
Points: 25
Position: No.8
Weight: 116kg
Caps: 28

JACK NOWELL

Club: Exeter Chiefs
Height: 1.81m
Debut: v France
Points:20
Position: Winger
Weight: 87kg
Caps: 9

GEOFF PARLING

Club: Exeter Chiefs
Height: 1.98m
Debut: v Scotland
Points: 5
Position: Lock
Weight: 117kg
Caps: 24

PLAYER PROFILES

CHRIS ROBSHAW

Club: Harlequins
Height: 1.88m
Debut: v Argentina
Points: 10
Position: Flanker
Weight: 109kg
Caps: 38

FLANKER

HENRY SLADE

Club: Exeter Chiefs
Height: 1.88m
Debut: v France
Points: 0
Position: Fly Half
Weight: 87kg
Caps: 1

FLY HALF

BILLY VUNIPOLA

Club: Saracens
Height: 1.88m
Debut: v Argentina
Points: 15
Position: No.8
Weight: 126kg
Caps: 18

NO.8

MAKO VUNIPOLA

Club: Saracens
Height: 1.80m
Debut: v Fiji
Points: 5
Position: Prop
Weight: 121kg
Caps: 22

PROP

ENGLAND RUGBY

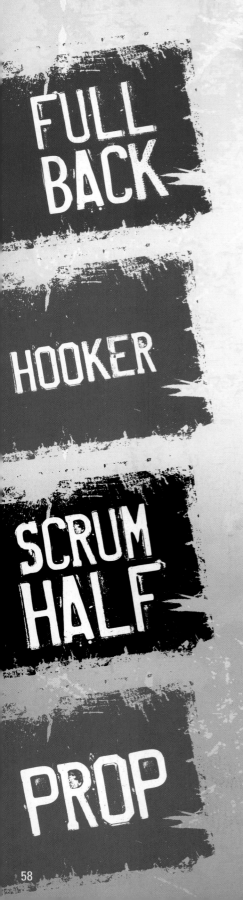

FULL BACK

HOOKER

SCRUM HALF

PROP

ANTHONY WATSON

Club: Bath Rugby
Height: 1.85m
Debut: v New Zealand
Points: 20
Position: Full Back
Weight: 93kg
Caps: 10

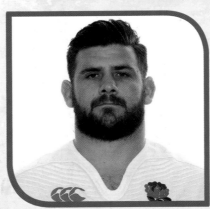

ROB WEBBER

Club: Bath Rugby
Height: 1.83m
Debut: v Italy
Points: 5
Position: Hooker
Weight: 116kg
Caps: 13

RICHARD WIGGLESWORTH

Club: Saracens
Height: 1.75m
Debut: v Italy
Points: 5
Position: Scrum Half
Weight: 86kg
Caps: 22

DAVID WILSON

Club: Bath Rugby
Height: 1.85m
Debut: v Argentina
Points: 5
Position: Prop
Weight: 125kg
Caps: 43

PLAYER PROFILES

TOM WOOD

Club: Northampton Saints
Height: 1.95m
Debut: v Wales
Points: 0
Position: Flanker
Weight: 107kg
Caps: 37

FLANKER

BEN YOUNGS

Club: Leicester Tigers
Height: 1.78m
Debut: v Scotland
Points: 45
Position: Scrum Half
Weight: 92kg
Caps: 48

SCRUM HALF

TOM YOUNGS

Club: Leicester Tigers
Height: 1.75m
Debut: v Fiji
Points: 0
Position: Hooker
Weight: 101kg
Caps: 23

HOOKER

QUIZ AND PUZZLE ANSWERS

P.26 GUESS WHO? ANSWERS

1. Alex Corbisiero
2. George Ford
3. Courtney Lawes
4. Billy Vunipola
5. Ben Youngs

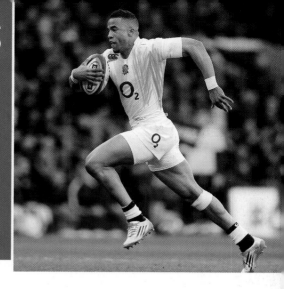

P.30 SPOT THE BALL

P.34–35 ENGLAND QUIZ

Question 1:   23
Question 2:   1987
Question 3:   82,000
Question 4:   Katy McLean
Question 5:   The Wallabies
Question 6:   Exeter Chiefs
Question 7:   Simon Amor
Question 8:   1871

Question 9:   St Lucia
Question 10:   St James Park
Question 11:   1986
Question 12:   Rory Underwood
Question 13:   Third place
Question 14:   South Africa, Australia and New Zealand have all won two each.
Question 15:   Ben Youngs and Jack Nowell

WHERE'S RUCKLEY?

He's in here somewhere, can you find him?